MICHAEL SCHERTZ

Guide to Photographing Mt. Rainier National Park – Vol 1

Text & photography Copyright©2014 by Michael Schertz,
except as noted

ISBN: 9780692352229
(StarHawk Publishing)

Editor: Kathy Nelson
Book Design & Cover Design: Michael Schertz
Layout: Michael Schertz

Cover Photo: "Resting Place", taken Mt. Rainier National Park, taken above Paradise on August 24, 2014

Important Please Read: Any of these locations identified in this book may require physical travel in remote areas or in conditions that elevate the potential risk of personal injury. It is always recommended that proper knowledge through training and experience is obtained prior to adventure. Travel to these locations at your own risk and always check conditions with the National Park Service prior to venturing out. The author and those involved in the publishing of this book decline all responsibility against injury, stranding, injury or getting lost. Additionally, the same are assume no responsibly against any kind of mishap as a result of adherence to advice or directions indicated in this book. Situations in the natural world are in constant state of change or the author or publisher do not take responsibility for outdated information, errors or omissions.

MICHAEL SCHERTZ

CONTENTS

ACKNOWLEDGMENTS

I want to acknowledge all those who have encouraged my photographs and my books. From the first days of clicking a shutter, you have supported my efforts and been there as I continue to improve.

To my children and grandchildren, our times together that have led to some of my favorite images and more memorable photo shoots must be acknowledged.

And last but not least to Kathy, whose support and belief in my art has been fuel for the creation of these books.

MICHAEL SCHERTZ

INTRODUCTION

There are few places in this country as amazing as our National Parks. I relocated to the Pacific Northwest over a decade ago for work. I quickly found my home to be in the foothills of the Cascade Mountains. I have had the opportunity to live just outside Mt. Rainier National Park for over the past 10 years. This was our fifth National Park in the land where John Muir tread. I had photographed my hiking adventures over the years and my passion grew as I photographed the Cascades lush green wilderness areas and especially those of Mount Rainier.

Being close to the park and within close proximity to Olympic North Cascades and other National Parks not only in the Northwest but even in the Rocky Mountains states has provided me with many amazing photographic experiences. It is through this that I have learned to connect with the earth and then in turn share that with others. The land is dynamic constantly changing never static. That is why I return to many of the same locations; different seasons at different times in the day, different weather conditions, different geologic changes and see a new photograph for the first time.

Mt. Rainier is not the only thing this park has to offer. I hope I am able to show you something a bit more to find and photograph in this park. For many folks who visit the park or any National Park for that matter, it is a rushed, traffic packed experience. While we all try to grapple with time and availability to experience and enjoy our natural wonders. It may be hard to believe that there are those who live in the shadow of this great National Park who have never visited it. Find a way to slow your pace and make the most of your time while there. There is so much to this park and taking in its beauty is a place to energize the soul. From the caps of ice that are resting on its top to the ribbons of streams and rivers that cut down the slopes, the forests that flourish on its slopes all coming together because of geology to make this amazing National Park. The waterfalls are each different and establish a character and a message for those who take the time to listen. When these flowing bodies of water reach a pocket, they form ponds or lakes of transparent amazement. These crystalline bodies of water can be alluring at times of the year, however they quickly make those who indulge aware of icy glaciers that feeds them.

Many visit Mount Rainier National Park each year and drive primarily to locations such as Paradise, Longmire and Sunrise. While each is a beautiful location there are miles and miles of trails and wilderness that goes unvisited by the public each year. Don't be afraid to park your car and venture to the wood line and you will find it is a rewarding experience and will provide you with a multitude of photographic opportunities. When you do leave your car for the trails keep in mind to go prepared. Plan and prepare so you are experiencing a safe and memorable adventure. While an amazing and wonderful location Mount Rainier National Park can present sudden weather changes and physical terrain challenges that should be taken into consideration. For example, getting your feet wet in a stream crossing or getting drenched in an unexpected storm can leave those unprepared with uncomfortable and potentially a dangerous hypothermic situation. Plan and take the appropriate gear and if necessary get training or go with those who are experienced in back country adventures.

MICHAEL SCHERTZ

PLANNING YOUR TRIP WITH THIS BOOK

Saying that the locations in this book are the best and only places to create images in Mt. Rainier National Park would be incorrect. There are thousands and thousands of places to capture amazing images within this amazing park. What I've attempted to do in this book is to provide a few ideas for locations that I repeatedly like to visit and photograph. Especially if you're visiting the park and your time is limited, this book will give you areas to visit and potentially spark some creative juices, allowing you to gather some memorable images to take home with you.

The park can be divided into two primary regions. The North and South sections. The book is focuses on the Northern section. The Northern section of the park includes Mowich Lake, Spray Falls, Ranger Falls, Tolmie Peak and Summerland as examples. Within the Northern section, the primary access into the park is in the North East corner of the park, through the White River area however there are other points of accesses to the park and their features warrant the time to visit them.

Subsequent volumes will focus on additional Northern locations and the Southern section. A great many visitors to the park enter through the Nisqually entrance. Many of the services available within the park are at Longmire and Paradise, which is found through the Nisqually entrance. Look for these locations in Volumes 2-3 and more.

Regardless of what section you choose to visit there are a variety of photo opportunities within the park. This book and subsequent volumes serve as a guide. Providing you with a set of recommendations to locations in the park that are destinations for great photo opportunities.

I don't have maps in the book, technology has changed so much and many of today's photographers utilize Global Positioning Systems (GPS) to drive directly to locations. With the pace of the world requiring us to identify and maximize our time by using these navigation devices. I have included the GPS coordinates for areas for you to begin your image compositions. In areas like West Side Road and Stevens Canyon Road, the coordinates are for the beginning of road. This is because there are so many image opportunities along the road.

Much of the park does not have cell phone access. So if you are going to need access to data from our device, make sure and download it prior to entering the park. There is some intermittent signal, but nothing that is reliable enough to ensure your safety.

PERSONAL GEAR

Hiking Gear

When spending time in the back country areas the appropriate personal gear is just as important as your photo gear. Making sure that you have adequately prepared can make for a pleasant and memorable photo adventure. It is not the intent of this book to provide you with detailed technical aspects of the gear that you will need to photograph in nature. The following information is to provide you with introductory information to point you in the right direction on what you will need at the very least to be safe and dry.

Clothing

In many of the outdoor circles there is a saying "cotton kills". This is very true when spending time in the mountains of the Pacific Northwest. Ensuring that you have the appropriate layers of the right material is essential. I have found hikers in distress wearing tennis shoes and blue jeans who had fallen through the snow into a hidden Creek. They were suffering from early hypothermia.

Dressing in layers is the key to safe dress in the back country. It allows you to add more layers when temperatures dip, and remove layers when perspiring or getting too hot. Materials consisting of content or cotton blends should not be in those layers.

Outer Wear

Your outerwear can be very important, especially when you adventure takes you miles from your vehicle. Alterations in the weather can come on suddenly and you will find that the right gear will keep you warm and dry. This turn can help you focus on the situation and can help you keep a clear head, which can make the difference in your safety.

Do your research and make sure that you have both a Shell Jacket but also the pants. Protect yourself as you would your camera. It is important to be comfortable and dry when out capturing photographs in nature. It gets tough to focus on the composition when you are shivering and you're miserable.

Also, a hood and a hat are important as well. Keeping your head dry and comfortable can assist in your hands keeping warm. Yes, your hands. If you don't understand that, do the research. Also, good gloves will putting the finishing touches on your protective shell system.

Footwear

Athletic shoes may work just fine when working around the car and taking pictures. But, when hiking a mile or two comes into play the need for better support and protection will be necessary. Having the right foot wear for the terrain can provide you with warmth, protection and support. Keep in mind what was said earlier, "Cotton can kill" and keep it off your feet. Look for synthetic socks or wool socks to envelop your feet before you stick them into your boots. I have a variety of boots for light hiking, backpacking, kayaking, climbing, rafting, snowshoeing and mountaineering. I don't like cranky feet when I am trying to be all Zen and capture great images.

Packs & Dry Bags

So you spend all that money to purchase your camera and equipment. You get your personal gear systems set up and you decide to use a cheap backpack to put it all in. You are 5 miles into your shoot and the straps are digging into your shoulders, and your back aches. Then suddenly a strap breaks and the weather suddenly goes very wrong with heavy winds and driving rain. Your attention goes to getting out of the situation and you try to head back to your vehicle. Your expense gear gets wet and you aching from the pack. These situations (they do happen, have been with folks when it goes wrong) may not all happen at once, but the point is that a quality pack with comfortable suspension and a dry bag to put in to mitigate from hazards.

10 essentials

Back in the 1930s a Seattle based organization comprised of mountaineers, climbers and other outdoor adventurers. You can find more details in the current edition of <u>Mountaineering: Freedom of the Hills</u> (see suggested reading section of this book). The original list of items called the ten essentials has since been modified. While it is good that you are aware of these, however if you aren't carrying them they won't be there when you need them.

1. Navigation (consists of map and compass)
2. Sun protection (consists of sunglasses and sunscreen)
3. Insulation (extra clothing, in dry container)
4. Illumination (headlamp/flashlight, with extra batteries)
5. First-aid supplies
6. Fire (waterproof matches/lighter/candles)
7. Repair kit and tools
8. Nutrition (extra food)
9. Hydration (extra water, in container)
10. Emergency shelter (for example, sheet of plastic or small tarp)

This has become a standard in the outdoor adventurer arena. I always have these with me when I head out to shoot photos. They are constantly in my car and any time I venture more than quarter mile or so from my car, they are with me in my pack.

Navigation

Being able to know where you are and where you

want to be is a pretty important aspect for capturing images off the beaten path. Not being able to find your way safely can increase the chance for you to become lost. With today's technologies we can have Global Positioning Systems (GPS) provide this direction and information to us. But to totally rely on higher technologies that can fail, can be very risky. Being able to read a map and perform basic navigation will important as a backup when on an adventure in the back country.

I invested several years ago in a personal locator beacon. Mine allows me to send messages to communicate that I am fine or in trouble. In a case of an emergency, it will notify Search and Rescue and provide them with valuable information as to where I am at. This is a great device to carry with on your adventures. While it won't keep you from harm's way, it will provide critical information to your support system to find you and get you out.

MICHAEL SCHERTZ

PHOTO GEAR

So there are a ton of books written about photography gear and the technical techniques to get great photos. I will not indicate a specific camera or other piece of equipment by brand, they change so very much and with all the capabilities out there with equipment today great images can be done with a DSLR, a point and shoot, or a camera phone.

This section is about what I have used to capture the images captured in this book. In turn hopefully provide you with some useable information of how to capture a workable image when photographing in this amazing park.

Camera
There is a variety of cameras in the marketplace today. With adequate practice each can deliver wonderful photographs. It is important to be sure that you are comparable with your camera and its technical capabilities if you want to ensure memorable quality images. So making sure that you practice, become familiar with and are comfortable with your camera prior to visiting Mt. Rainier National Park is very important.

If you are hiking with your camera, make sure that you have a strap or a method to carry it to reduce the risk of damage from it hitting rocks or trees. Also making sure you have adequate batteries and storage space or film is important to make sure that you can capture.

Lenses

Many of today's digital cameras come with fixed lenses. They can adjust from zoom to wide-angle and meet most people's needs. But there are others who carry the DSLR and cameras that have interchangeable lenses. In those cases it is asked important to have the right lenses to capture the images that you want. When shooting the landscapes in the park my camera bag has a telephoto (up to 300mm), a wide angle (XX mm), and ultra wide angle (10-22mm) lenses.

This combination of lenses allows me to adapt to a variety of situations and allows me to compose and create images that are memorable. Now while I have larger lenses for photographing wildlife up close I can generally capture the images that present with the telephoto lens. If I'm going for a specific wildlife shoot I will unpack my large telephoto lenses to get up close and personal to the wildlife.

Tripods

Now tripods can be a must when shooting great photos and there are as many options as there are camera options out there. As with camera's they also come in a variety of price tags. I tend to shoot with a carbon fiber tripod that allows me to hike it into locations without too much excess weight, but it did require me to save my pennies to purchase it. Which required me to shoot with a variety of other types that I picked up from various places, until I could purchase what I have and enjoy using today. But selecting a tripod that is appropriate for your camera is important and it is just as important to practice with it prior to your exploring the park.

At the very least the tripod you select must accomplish the following:

- Allow your camera to securely mount to the tripod
- Allow for vertical as well as horizontal positioning
- Ensure that the tripod can support the weight of the camera/lens
- Safeguard that the camera can pivot 360 degrees
- Can collapse and can be carried easily
- Light enough for you to carry at least a mile

Whatever you choose as a tripod, make sure it works for you. You might chose to shoot handheld only and that is fine, but it will seriously limit you to the photo opportunities that photographing in this park will provide to you.

Flash

Typically I shoot with just the ambient light. It requires me to shoot on tripod and long exposure times. However, there is a use for a flash. You don't necessarily need a separate flash or extension cables. I will on occasion do fill flash on some image compositions. Both of the DSLR bodies I shoot with have a pop up flash that while it does present with limitations, works great for the fill flash purpose.

Some however, will try to lighten up in post-production of their images. This can work, however it can also make aspects of your image appear grainy and it can be avoided with a bit of flash at the time you shoot the image.

Bean Bags

There will be situations where the tripod won't quite get the camera in the position you want to get capture the composition you wanted. It is in those situation that I reach down in my pack and pull out my bean bag. Though I have a commercially made one now, I have used and wore out a homemade one for years. These are pretty low tech but can be a very useful tool that warrants a place in your bag.

Cable Release

Now some will say that if you are going to shoot from a tripod you must absolutely use a cable release or remote trigger. I can say that this is not entirely true. Controlling my breathing and with a steady hand, I click on the tripod and capture crisp images repeatedly. But when it is dark, foggy or situations where I don't believe I can carry off the image with triggering the shutter with my finger, I will attach a release. I have remote, cable and interval releases that I carry with me each time I am photographing in the park, so that I am ready in any situation that may present.

Conditions in the mountains can change quickly and abruptly, so being ready with a release that will allow you to trigger your camera to the optimal shot is worth taking the time in bringing one.

Rain protection

Just as important as ensuring you have enough battery power in your camera, making sure you have rain protection is essential when you are photographing in Mt. Rainier National Park. There are many different covers for cameras in the marketplace today, at a variety of prices. As long as they do the job they are designed to do, to keep you camera out of the rain then they are good. I have seen everything from zip seal kitchen bags and trash bags with a whole cut in it all the way to the tailored covered. I have several different covers, they aren't overly expensive, but they do the trick. Just don't find yourself out capturing images and get caught in a downpour or the misty haze of a cloud (all common in the park) without some protection for your camera and lens.

Batteries

There is little as frustrating as getting ready to take your photos and realizing the batteries in your camera are dead. Making sure that you have the batteries charged in your camera is essential. It also doesn't hurt to have at least one set of backup batteries. But if you're going for a multi-day shoot it may be part of your planning to ensure you have multiple batteries or a method to charge them available to you. Because at the end of the day if you don't have the battery power you are NOT taking pictures. Having had the challenge of running out of battery, each of my cameras now has a dual battery pack to ensure that doesn't happen. I also carry at least one to two complete backups, to ensure I have enough battery power.

Keep in mind that in the winter months and when you are shooting around the freeze line on the mountain. Batteries can drain much faster in the cold temperatures. Plan accordingly for such conditions.

Memory

In the same category as battery power, when that moment comes for that amazing sunset and your camera memory is full, your frustration can peak quickly. Whether you are shooting JPEG or RAW, ensuring that you have sufficient memory to capture all the moments and all the images is important for a successful photo shoot. If you have traveled any distance to get to the park it can be a great move to ensure that you have a little bit more memory than you planned. It gives you a buffer for all the images that will present themselves.

Once you have those memory cards full, having a way to download those images safely and easily at the end of your shoot is also important. Having a card reader to download directly to your PC or to a portable drive of some sort can help ensure the safeguarding of the images. I keep an 8 gigabyte card as a buffer when I am out shooting, just in case something happens and I need that little something more to capture it.

Carrying It All

Carrying camera gear around can get heavy, awkward and result in broken camera gear or items lost. There are a variety of packs, harnesses, and slings available in the marketplace today. It is totally up to your personal choice how you wish to carry your gear around. I have used harness systems on days when I shoot handheld. I also frequently breakdown one of my bigger camera bags and place gear into a smaller backpack when hiking into the back country. Carrying a conventional camera strap has resulted in things breaking for me so I tend not to use them. Practice with the system before-hand and find something that works for you. Don't wait until you get to the park to try out your choice.

Other Accessories

There are a ton of accessories available in the marketplace today, designed to make a photographer's life more convenient and easy. However, all things considered you have determine if they truly directly contribute to the. So you choose what you must have, since you have to carry it all when you venture from the car.

NORTHERN LOCATIONS

Mt. Rainier is the centerpiece of the park. This 14,000+ foot peak captures the eye of every visitor. When accessing the northern locations, visitors will find entrances at White River, Mowich or Carbon River. White River is the north east gate, Mowich and Carbon River on the northwest corners. If you wish to drive and explore the northern locations you have to enter multiple entrances to be accessed. This is due to no roads connecting east to the west aspects of the northern section. If you want to explore the Mowich Lake and other aspects of the northwest segment of the park, entrance of the park will need to be done through the town of Wilkerson and following Highway 165. If coming into the park via this route, be aware that a large portion of this road is not paved. In the dryer seasons in Washington (yes, it does not always rain) this can create a very dusty experience. By late morning, during the summer months you can expect to meet dozens of vehicles who are sharing your thoughts about exploring this portion of the park. This can take dust to level which you may not have expected. Also, keep in mind if you are wanting to drive a convertible vehicle with the top down you will have the distinct taste of dust in your mouth and if you are silly enough to park your car along the side of the road (usually the only option when visiting this entrance) and leave the top down or windows down, you will return to find a significant film of dust layer across your upholstery.

This road is not open all year round. There is a gate at the border of the park on Highway 165 which closes when the snows arrive and does not open until that snow melts out. First snows can begin to accumulate around Thanksgiving which will close the gate and not open in late May and in some cases as late as later July. Tied directly to the impact of the winter seasons snowfall. When your plans have you wanting to explore the north east segment of the park you enter through the White River entrance. Taking Highway 410 into the park, you will drive approximately 5 miles on the Mather Memorial Highway. At 5 miles the road splits. Following the signs and taking the road to the right will take you to the White River Entrance and the Wilderness Information Center. From there, it is 16 miles approximately to arrive at the Sunrise Visitors Center.

As with the northwest entrance into this region of the park, it is not open year around. The White River gate will close when the snows get heavy. Much of the roads in the north region are in the shade and snow can linger longer than those areas facing south which will melt out faster. When it is open, it is a popular entry to the park and thousands will enter and visit the park through this gate. So if you wish to not deal with large groups of people, plan accordingly. There are several months after Labor Day where attendance drops significantly and the weather is great. There are numerous day hikers who enter the park so it is easy to meet visitors from around the world on any day. Plan on arriving early for better parking options and fewer crowds. I like shooting in the early mornings since the light is optimal and the crowds are less.

MICHAEL SCHERTZ

Ranger Falls

GPS Coordinates for Image: N46 59.040 W121 51.239
Elevation: 2791 ft
Optimal Times of Year: Summer / Fall
Accessibility: Moderate hike
Gear recommendations:

- Photography equipment
- Hiking gear for a light trail
- 10 essentials

Description:
If you suffer from creaky knees or don't have the endurance for a strenuous hike, this trail is your ticket. The gentle incline will bring you about a mile to the falls. The water flow of the falls it totally dependent on the time of year that you do this hike. Spring and early summer can bring heavy flows from snowpack melting, then diminishing flows in the summer. Autumn begins an increasing flow and the cycle repeats. If you wish to continue from the falls, Green Lake is a little further up the trail.

Since the floods of 2006, entry at the Carbon River entrance of the park has changed. Visitors must now Park at the entrance and then hike or mountain bike to their trailheads where they used to be able to drive. From the entrance it is approximately 2 miles to the trail head and from there you can begin the hike.

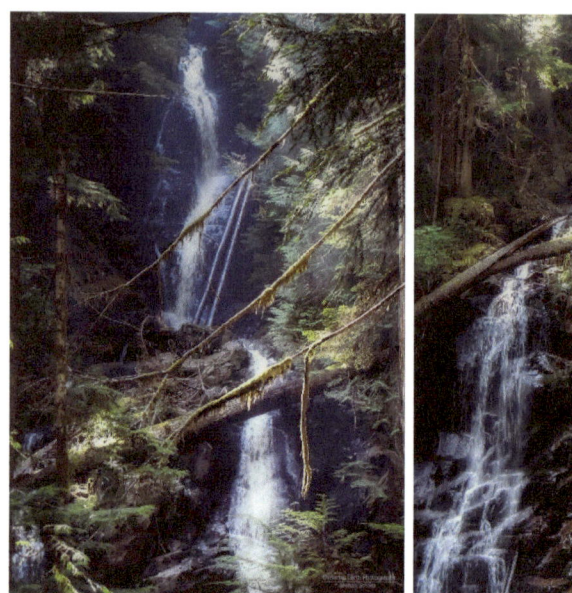
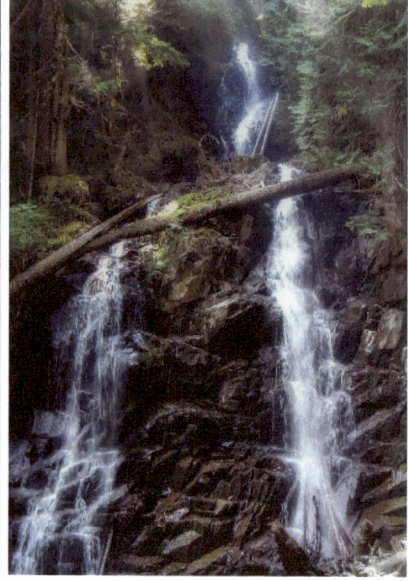

Story Behind the Image
There has been much that has changed since the floods of 2006; nature is dynamic and always changing. My favorite images from this location were taken prior to the flood and while I debated on which images to use, I selected these.

Hiking with my children and now grandchildren are moments of great lifting of my spirit. These images are no exception and from one of those moments. I had been hiking with my two youngest children, we were taking in an early Saturday morning hike. We had noticed a little haze when we started the hike, but combined with a bit of fog it did not stand out to me. The smell of smoke in the air, I attributed to area campers. It was a great morning hike and we arrived at the falls after a nice hike up in elevation.

While at the falls we noticed that the wind had shifted and the smoke seemed to be getting heavier. I was able to snap this photo among others before we decided to head back down the trail. Once we arrived at the car, we realized by the helicopters, the heavy smoke and the trees exploding in flames across the Carbon River that a forest fire was in full swing. We watched from the road for close to an hour as fire fighters and helicopters worked the fire line. It was a dynamic close to a Saturday morning hike.

MICHAEL SCHERTZ

Mowich Lake

GPS Coordinates for Image: N46 55.989 W121 51.831

Elevation: 4917 ft.

Optimal Times of Year: Summer / Fall (winter if willing to snowshoe)

Accessibility: Easy drive in shoot, trails around the lake is also an easy hike

Gear recommendations:

- Photography equipment
- Hiking gear
- If winter adventure, snowshoes or x-country skis
- 10 essentials

Description:

Accessing the lake is easy by vehicle during the months when the road is open. When the gates at the park edge are closed getting to the lake can be a bit more challenging. Winter time can require use of cross-country skis or snowshoes once the snow begins to fall. There is approximately 15 miles of gravel road that will need to be navigated in order to get to the lake. Summers can be dry and roads are unpaved and become dusty and blankets your car with a nice layer of dirt. Arriving early will be important due to the popularity of this location when the gate is open. Although I have never felt threatened or scared I have encountered bears in this area on a couple of occasions. Bear spray would be recommended.

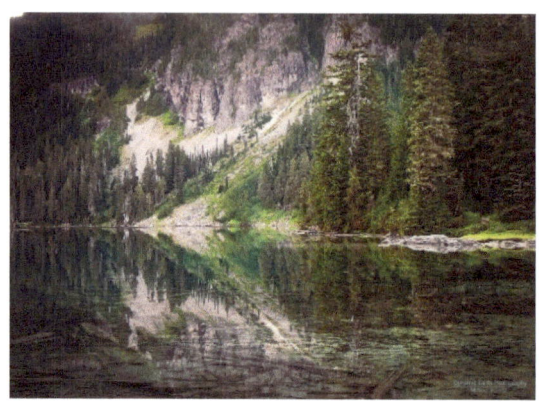

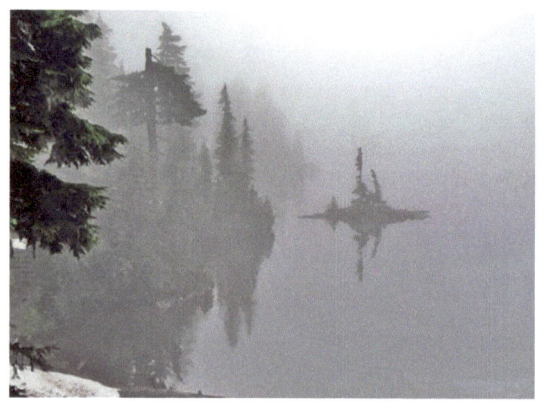

Story Behind the Image

I have hiked and photographed Mowich Lake many times over the years. There are a variety of relatively easy means to access the lake. They include by car, mountain bike and hiking in the warmer months to x-country skiing or snowshoeing in the winter months when the road it closed. From the town of Buckley, a few miles out of town the road transitions from paved to gravel. I have learned over the years that the best time of the day to visit this portion of the park is either on days when the weather may not be optimal (cloudy, overcast, or foggy) or very early in the morning before the masses begin to arrive. The majority of people who visit this area tend to be locals, however it is not exclusive and non-locals do find their way there.

Arriving at the lake to capture the first light of the day or to be there on an overcast day when the lake is glassy and flat is optimal. These two particular images occurred on two separate photo shoots.

The first photo of the crystal clear waters of the lake in the reflection of the mountain was taken on an early morning shoot with several photography friends. The soft light of the morning and the glassy surface of the lake provided great shots. The lake side of the mountain shielded the direct sunlight. This soft light made for an optimal situation to shoot around this lake. In the early morning, the water for a short period of time can present as glass. It is during these times that you can capture so many different photo opportunities. Once the sun crests over the ridge, the light will become harsh and there will be significantly greater contrast. Also, the most subtle of breezes can ripple the lake and diminish your photo opportunities.

Fog in the northwest is pretty common. Fog within Mt. Rainier National Park is also quite common. It can present some amazing photo opportunities. This second image is of Mowich Lake and fog had taken possession of the day. The shoot was to hike and photograph from Mowich up a portion of the Spray Park Trail. I started shooting this image at the lake, then made my way up the trail, all in the fog. I provided me with several opportunities and this image of the lake reminds me of how the fog can present a very different energy than when it is clear, sunny or even cloudy.

Spray Falls Trail

GPS Coordinates for Image: (trail head) N46 55.837 W121 51.745
Elevation: 4943 ft
Optimal Times of Year: Summer / Fall
Accessibility: Moderately strenuous hike
Gear recommendations:

- Photography equipment
- Hiking gear
- 10 essentials

Description:

Spray Falls trail begins at Mowich Lake and makes its way to Spray Park. This hike is not what I would call challenging or difficult, but does take time. All along this trail there are drainages, seeps, creeks and streams. Since there is not a tremendous amount of strong light that gets through the tree canopy, most of the rocks are covered with heavy moss. This can present a multitude of great photo opportunities, along the trail. I prefer to shoot along this trail in the early morning or on an overcast day. It provides the best light options and keeps the bright white light spots from messing up my images. You may not get to trails end, but take your time and have your tripod ready because to get that flowing water images you will need a steady platform to shoot from and longer shutter time.

Considerations accessing the trailhead are the same as those for getting to Mowich Lake. This can be a particularly fond area to shoot when fog sits along the trail. As with Mowich Lake this can become a very popular area in the warmer months. Arrive early to get good parking and allow you to avoid the crowds. If camping ensure that you have a permit. Information for camping in the Park can be found on the National Park Service website for Mount Rainier. While I have never felt threatened I have encountered bears while photographing in this area a couple of times. It may be advisable to have bear spray with you and be prepared in how to use it.

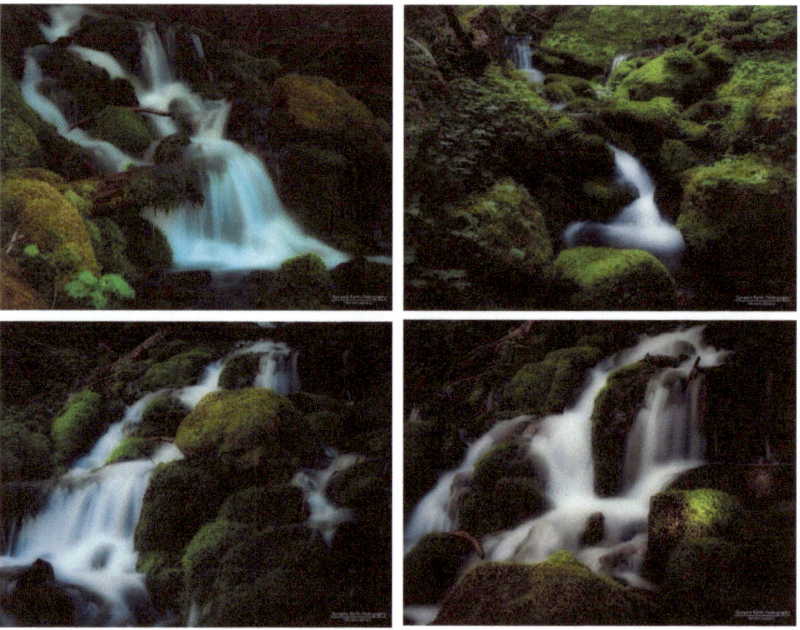

Story Behind the Image

The trail to Spray Park is a very popular one in the late summer when the wildflowers are in bloom. Due to the state terrain, the abundant moisture, and the glaciers on the mountain there are numerous small creeks, drainages and seeps all along this trail that provide a multitude of photo opportunities. You'll notice on a map of this trail there is a side trail that provides a short excursion to Spray Falls. Just prior to this junction is a small creek which provides a variety of photo opportunities. Due to the heavy canopy it does not fall into the sunlight until late morning or early afternoon. I have photographed this cascade many times and it is truly one of my favorite.

On this particular occasion several friends joined me for a shoot of areas along the Spray Park trail. We had started photographing before sunrise at Mowich Lake and had arrived at this location in late morning. Taking our time to photograph the multitude of creeks, drainages and seeps that are found along the trail, slowed our pace. Due to the heavy tree canopy and shelter from the mountain, it allowed us to have ample time and provided shaded light late in the morning. However it does restrict some of your options due to white spots of sunlight that do fall along the flowing water.

When photographing flowing water like these I will

work from side to side and bottom to top as time permits to capture the images of the location. When shooting with a group be familiar with each other's shooting styles and communicate as you work so everyone knows their position and what is occurring with each person on the team. This was a cool summer morning at the hot sun had not pierced through the leaves of the tree canopy and afforded us ample time to work through each shot.

Spray Park

GPS Coordinates for Image: N46 54.924 W121 46.535
Elevation: 6027 ft
Optimal Times of Year: Late Summer / Fall
Accessibility: Moderately strenuous hike
Gear recommendations:

- Photography equipment
- Hiking gear
- 10 essentials

Description:

There are backpackers that hike through this area each year. But the key time of year that attracts visitors is in late July through August when the wildflowers burst into bloom. This is when most of the visitors explore these high country meadows. Combined with Mt. Rainier in the background it can present with great opportunities. Foggy days, which are common, can present interesting lighting, but limits the views of the mountain. There can be several feet of snow residing in these upper meadows well into early August that will impact which flowers bloom when. When hiking and photographing in this high country be prepared. Be aware of weather conditions; they can change quickly so it is important to be prepared not only for your camera, but also your personal safety.

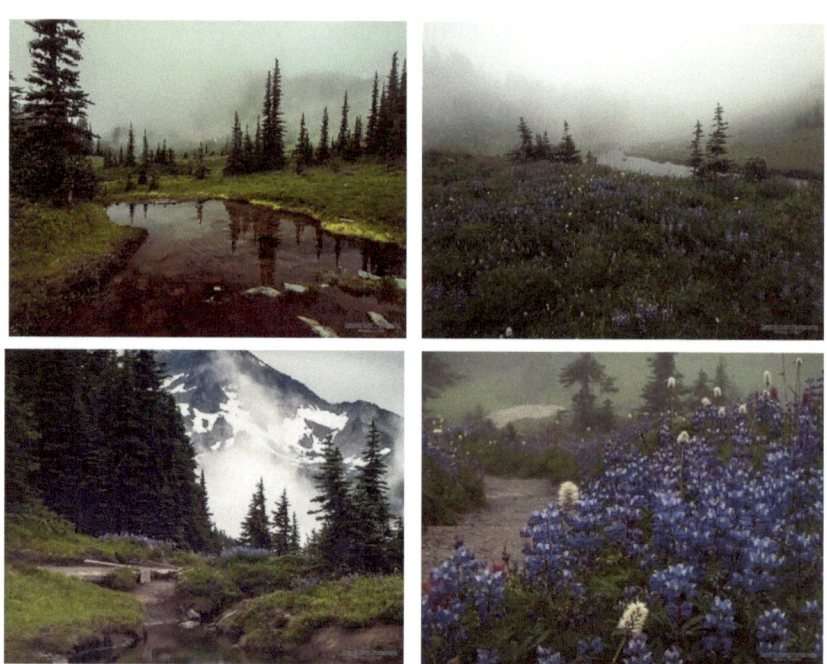

Story Behind the Image

I have hiked to Spray Falls many times, it is a hike you plan for and accommodate for "stuff that happens". Many of those times have caused me to abandon the trek due to emergent weather changes. At time when I have made it to the meadows it has been quite foggy. Expecting it to burn off, most times for me it has not. However, it has provided me with wildflowers, fog and enjoyable shoots.

These images are from a shoot a few years ago which

started out foggy but after about 45 minutes became very windy and the fog changed to driving rain with elements of sleet. I had arrived at Mowich Lake at approximately 5:30 AM and made my way up the trail. It was hard for me to stay focused on the objective of Spray Park, I like to shoot images of flowing water but did not want to get distracted and not make it to my destination. I arrived a few hours later and began composing my images. As the morning continued, the fog remained and I continued to compose my images. By midmorning a light drizzle began to fall and a breeze began to blow. It wasn't long before the breeze turned into a strong wind which made photographing very challenging. As I began to gather up my gear and call it a good photo shoot, the drizzle transitioned to driving rain.

I quickly donned raingear for myself and my camera gear. I grabbed my trekking poles and began my descent back to my car. It is important to note that when hiking along steep grades and mountainsides the trails are not always flat. The uneven terrain and draining water when mixed with earth can present muddy and quite treacherous slick conditions. It is in these situations that I have found trekking poles to be useful in sustaining my footing. After a couple of hours I was able to make my way back to my car and make my way back home. I spent the rest of the day processing my images while the rain kept coming down. I can't think of a better way to spend the day.

Spray Falls

GPS Coordinates for Image: N46 54.934 W121 50.540
Elevation: 5119 ft
Optimal Times of Year: Summer / Fall
Accessibility: Moderately strenuous hike
Gear recommendations:

- Photography equipment
- Hiking gear
- 10 essentials

Description:
In order to get to this location you will need to access Mowich Lake and then hike around 2.5 miles of the Spray Park trail to get to the junction for the short trail that leads to Spray Falls. The trail ends at the falls and caution must be exercised in photographing this location. Many hike this trail in the summer months to feel the cool spray of the falls. However, the ground where the trail meets the river is eroded, rocky and constantly in change by Mother Nature. The current from the river is fast-moving; rocks can be slick and extreme caution is not exercised while shooting at this location a slip that results in injury or worse could occur.

As with any waterfall, debris that falls into the current of the water above the falls will make its way down. It is not uncommon for large rocks and even boulders to find their way down being pushed by the water of the falls. In the spring lingering snows can make it difficult to access the falls as well as spray Park. When this snows melt out water flows will still present an increased risk if you were to fall in the water. By midsummer water levels reduce bringing out distinct patterns in the falls and great composition possibilities for your images. It also makes it a little safer to move around the falls. As with any large falls and this one is around 350 feet, there is a breeze at the base of the falls. It is wise to be prepared for this mist. This can soak you, camera and gear. It can also make capturing images challenging.

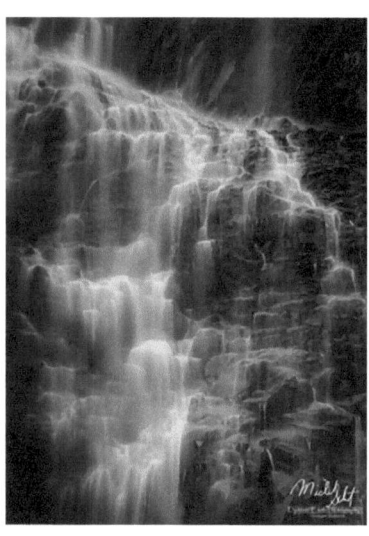
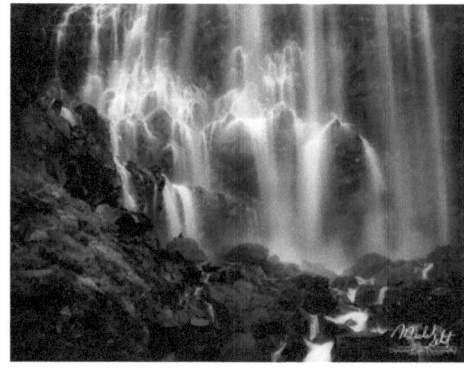

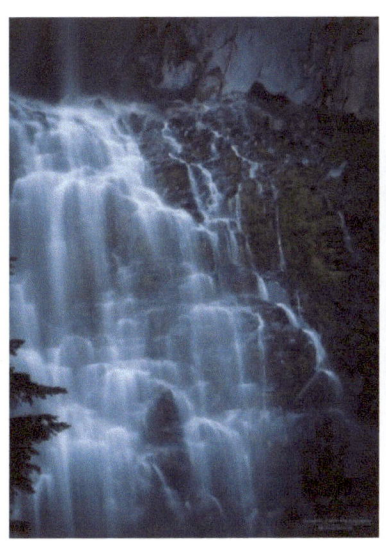
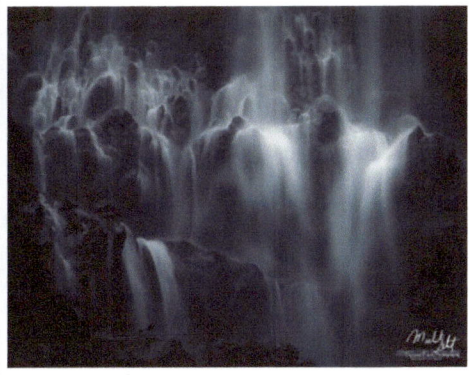

The Story Behind the Image

It was mid-August and I had arrived midmorning at Mowich Lake. Later than I had wanted but the day was overcast and the light was not harsh. I took my time shooting, stopping periodically to shoot along the drainages and small creeks on the trail. I noticed that the spray drift from the falls was moving to the right of the falls. I tried to make my way up the left side which required a little bushwhacking to get the camera angles I wanted. I also work from the side of the river. I noticed that the spray at times begin to lessen and I thought it may provide some opportunities to shoot on the right side of the river. I went downstream and found a natural bridge, in a log, to cross to the other side. It is important to note that there is no man-made means to the other side of the river. I made my way up the right side of the river composing images as I went. I had put my camera and myself in rain gear.

Ensuring footing on this side of the river was far more challenging with the spray regularly coating the rocks and grasses. The muddy terrain made it quite easy to stumble and slip. I made my way with caution up the slope toward the falls. I located several great compositions and waited for the mist to subside. I found myself waiting at times 20 minutes for the spray to lift for just a minute or two so I could snap a few frames. Standing in the mist isn't like standing in a fog bank on a misty morning; this mist is from water that is falling several hundred feet and comes with some force.

You see this falls is unique, it is two major steps. The first falls and then turns 90 degrees and the larger step falls and that is what is in these images. This is a fun shoot and one I enjoy doing each year. However, it is also a challenging photo shoot as the terrain can be steep, rocky, wet and slippery any time you're there to photograph.

GUIDE TO PHOTOGRAPHING MT.RAINIER
NATIONAL PARK – VOL1

Tolmie Peak

GPS Coordinates for Image: (trail head) N46 56.276 W121 52.029
Elevation: 4959 ft
Optimal Times of Year: Summer / Fall
Accessibility: Moderate hike
Gear recommendations:

- Photography equipment
- Hiking gear
- 10 essentials

Description:
After the floods of 2006, accessing this trail has become a bit more challenging. With the inability to drive further in at the Carbon River entrance to the park, it requires a hike or mountain bike ride of around 6 miles just to get to the trail head to begin the trek to the Tolmie Peak trail via the Insput Creek trail. Now if you want to go straight there you can drive to Mowich Lake and take a more direct route. The hike from Mowich is around 7.5 miles round trip. It is not a difficult hike; there is a slight ridge to hike down to get to Eunice Lake. There is also an old fire tower present that will provide some great photo opportunities.

Getting to this location may require parking and hiking longer or mountain biking to the trail head just to begin this hike. if you come in through the Carbon River Entrance. Honestly, I would take the Mowich Lake option. It is not overly difficult and the light through the trees can be inspirational and make for great photo opportunities.

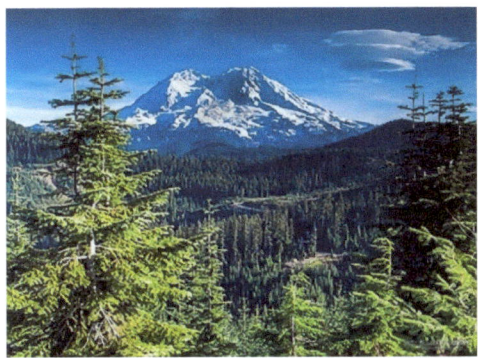

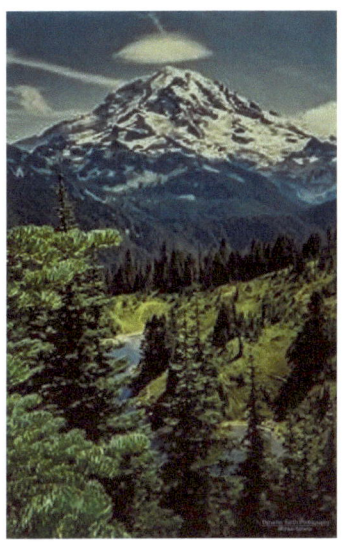

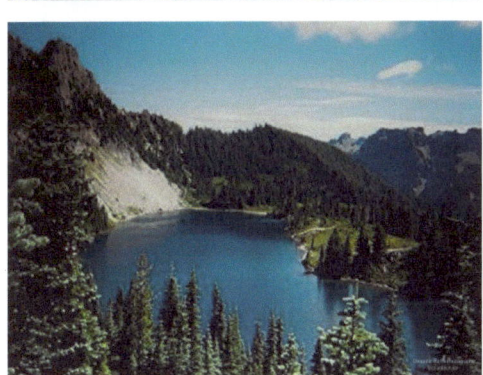

Story Behind the Image

There are so many trails that I have hiked and photographed with my children over the years. This hike is one of those that has a special memory for me. It was late on a summer morning when we started on the trail. My companions for this hike were my oldest and youngest daughters, the plan was to make it a day of exploration. The weather was clear and warm and it was what most would call a beautiful day. We parked at Mowich Lake and made our way north on the trail toward Eunice Lake and Tolmie Peak.

While not crowded, it is a popular trail, especially with young families. We did not find it a difficult trail to hike and even though the day was warm, the shade of the tree canopy made it comfortable. Along the way we met an 80 year old man hiking this trail with his grandchildren and great grandchildren. He hiked this trail like he had been doing it daily; it was truly inspiring watching him in action.

These images were captured on the ridge overlooking Eunice Lake. From this ridge it was a hike down to the lake and then on a bit further to the old fire tower that is on this trail. This short climb is about the most challenging aspect of the hike, but I would not consider it tremendously demanding.

Summerland

GPS Coordinates for Image: N46 51.875 W121 39.689

Elevation: 5954 ft

Optimal Times of Year: Summer / Fall

Accessibility: Strenuous hike

Gear recommendations:

- Photography equipment
- Hiking gear or backpacking gear (if going overnight)
- 10 essentials

Image Description:

This is not a technical hike to get to this location, but it will take time. This can make it a bit strenuous. From the White River parking lot at the campground, the trek to Summerland is roughly 4.5 miles. The snows will fall early here and will linger until late in the summer. But when the snow melts, the wildflowers can be expected. You may want to consider backpacking into this area and making it at least an overnight. This is a high demand campground and preparation to secure permits will be required, especially during the time when wildflowers are in bloom. Be prepared and plan for this one; it can be a rewarding adventure if properly prepared for.

This site can provide great photo opportunities with its meadows of wildflowers in the summer, but you also have great waterfalls, glaciers and mountain peak views all at your disposal for some amazing compositions.

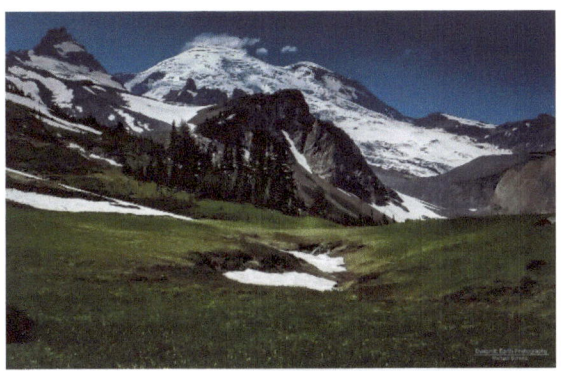

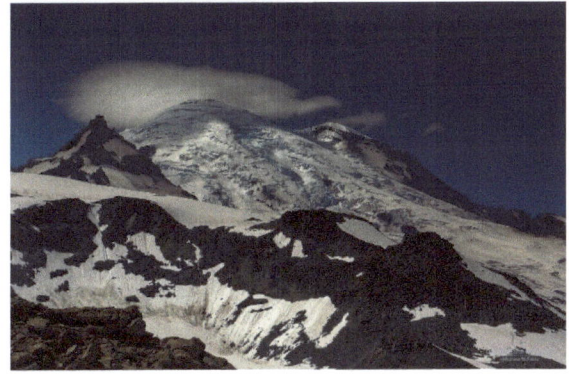

Story Behind the Image

There are a series of images that I have taken that are not from what I would call destination photo shoots. They are images captured during a longer adventure.

My second son and I were backpacking along the

Wonderland Trail. We had started at Longmire, going counter clockwise on this giant loop trail and we arrived at Summerland on day 3. Our camp the night before had been at Indian Bar and the hike from there had been an exercise in hiking up. I learned some hard lessons about camera weight, what is really needed and "stuff" that I carried and never used. The climb over Panhandle Gap was slushy and snowy. It was slow progress to the top of the gap, looking down over Summerland and realizing the "up" portion of our hike was about to end brought a smile to my face.

Once we made it down to the green grass, the packs came off and we checked out the amazing scenery of the area. This was a tough place for me to leave; it is very beautiful and I could easily stay a week. After our break, we made our way back on the trail. There was a few series of switchbacks and then the trail levels out. So remember if you are coming from White River it will be a slow climb to the switchbacks to get up to Summerland. For us our camp for the night was at White River. I would like to say it was a dry night, but rain became our friend that night requiring that all the gear stayed dry. Keeping our gear dry was the priority.

GUIDE TO PHOTOGRAPHING MT.RAINIER NATIONAL PARK – VOL1

White River

GPS Coordinates for Image: N46 54.141 W121 38.489
Elevation: 4243 ft
Optimal Times of Year: Summer / Fall
Accessibility: Drive in area
Gear recommendations:

- Photography equipment
- Hiking gear (if you want to venture away from the paved places)

Image Description:
When you enter the park through the White River entrance of the park you will find the turn off for the White River campground. From the junction it is another mile to the campground area. There is also a parking area used by climbers heading up Camp Schurman or backpackers hiking on the trails (more specifically the Wonderland). This also your launch point to hike to Summerland, as previously mentioned.

At White River, you are at a lower elevation and there are shots in the forest and shooting up the drainages and rivers toward the mountain.

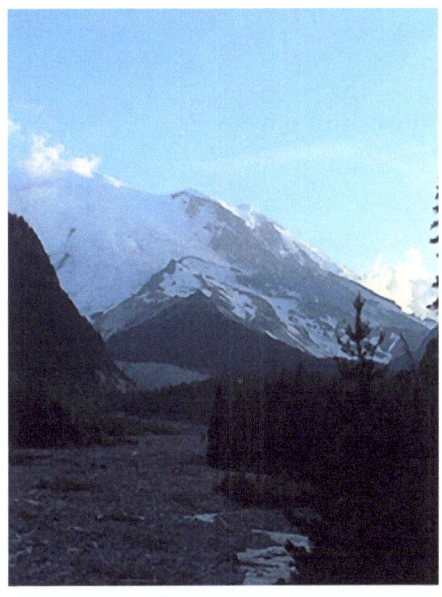

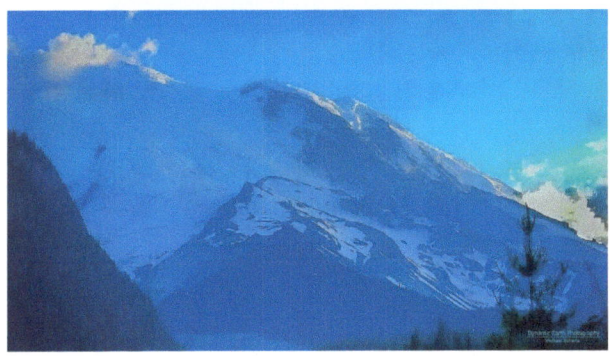

Story Behind the Image

As with the Summerland location, I hiked into this location from a trek on the Wonderland Trail. My second son and I camped here on Day 4. I have since driven here a number of times, but these images were taken during that trek.

It was late in the afternoon when we arrived at White River to camp. We would have likely been there several hours earlier, but we enjoyed ourselves relaxing at Summerland longer than we probably should have. The sky was relatively clear when we arrived, but this was not to last. Camp was established and a bit of relaxing and removal my boots were some happy moments. It was at this point that we noticed that an injury was starting to become a bit more pronounced and would soon cut our trip short. Injuries to feet and knees can cut a trip short as in our case.

As the day began to wind down I began shooting as the light became softer. Note to self, aligning personal energy level to photo shooting can allow for less mistakes. I was dragging from a long day of backpacking. At least for me, I was in the automatic mode with camera. I ended up deleting many of the images from this shoot. I also convinced myself that

I will wait until morning to finish and get the first light of the morning.   Soon after these images I crawled into my tent, hunkered into my sleeping back only to be awakened by the pelting of rain on my tent in the middle of the night. A storm had moved in and dumped on us during the night. When morning arrived the rain was lighter, but photo opportunities had diminished.

We packed up our gear and headed up the 2000 feet vertical gain in elevation to Sunrise. I had developed several large blisters on my feet and my son had significant swelling in one of his knees.
At that point our injuries overcame us and we elected to make a call and get a ride home.

Credits

Photographs

Each image in this book was taken by Michael Schertz and is copyrighted to him. Any utilization, alteration, copying, repackaging or repurposing of any image in this book without written authorization of the photographer is expressly forbidden.

Text

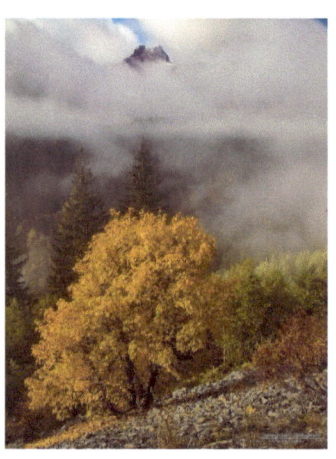

All text found in this volume has been written by the author and cannot be used without written authorization of the author.

Contact Information

To contact the author or see additional images go to:

Email - dynamic-earth@rainierconnect.com

Website / blog and online gallery can be found at
www.dynamic-earth-photos.com

Find us and check us out on Facebook *or* Google+

GUIDE TO PHOTOGRAPHING MT.RAINIER
NATIONAL PARK – VOL1

Suggested Websites

The Mt. Rainier Trail Conditions Site
http://www.nps.gov/mora/planyourvisit/trails-and-backcountry-camp-conditions.htm

Mt. Rainier Backcountry Camping and Reservations
http://www.nps.gov/mora/planyourvisit/wilderness-camping-and-hiking.htm

Mt. Rainier Road Conditions
http://www.nps.gov/mora/planyourvisit/road-status.htm

Mt. Rainier Recreational Weather Forecast
http://www.atmos.washington.edu/data/rainier_report.html

Trail Map for Mt. Rainier
http://www.nps.gov/mora/planyourvisit/upload/mount%20rainier%20park%20map.pdf

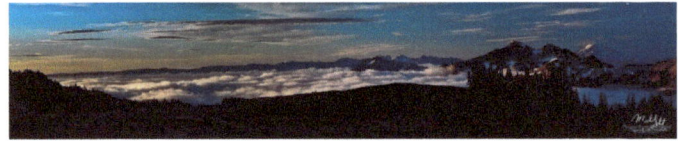

GUIDE TO PHOTOGRAPHING MT.RAINIER
NATIONAL PARK – VOL1

Suggested Reading

In order to better prepare for photographing in Mt. Rainier National Park, you may find information in the following books useful.

Photography
Digital Photography Outdoors
James Martin
The Mountaineers Books, 2007

Mastering Landscape Photography
Alain Briot
Rocky Nook, Inc, 2007

National Audubon Society Guide to Photographing National Parks
Tim Fitzharris
Firefly Books, 2009

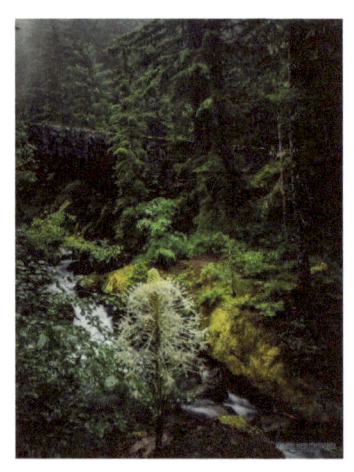

Outdoor Skills
Mountain Weather
Jeff Renner
The Mountaineers Books, 2005

Wilderness Basics
The San Diego Chapter of the Sierra Club

GUIDE TO PHOTOGRAPHING MT.RAINIER
NATIONAL PARK – VOL1

The Mountaineers Books, 2004

Mountaineering: The Freedom of the Hills
Edited by Ronald C. Eng
The Mountaineers Books, 2010

About the Author

Michael has been backpacking and hiking trails around the world for over 25 years. The last 15 years he has had a camera in his hands trying to capture the beauty 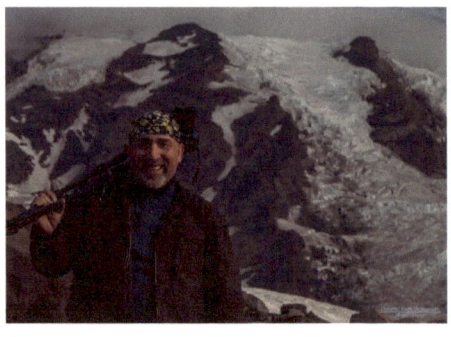 present in the places he visits. It is through the creativity and composition utilizing his camera that he is able to capture and create fine art images and books of this dynamic earth.

Whether in slot canyons and deserts of the southwest or in the deep snow high in the Rocky's or Cascades he is looking for that moment when light and environment come together in a special moment.

It is his aspiration to share those captured moments with the world. To communicate the ever changing beauty and delicacy of nature, the necessity to cherish these wild places and encourage each of us to get out and experience nature and share it with others as our birthright is his passion.

GUIDE TO PHOTOGRAPHING MT.RAINIER
NATIONAL PARK – VOL1